Lynn & Morgan

Enjoy the book!

Steve

2020:
A Perspective in Rhyme

by Steve Rosen

RoseDog❧Books
PITTSBURGH, PENNSYLVANIA 15238

RoseDog Books
585 Alpha Drive
Suite 103
Pittsburgh, PA 15238
Visit our website at *www.rosedogbookstore.com*

ISBN: 978-1-6366-1041-2
eISBN: 978-1-6366-1099-3

2020:

A Perspective in Rhyme

Table of Contents

State of the Union Entering 2020

After three years of the Trump presidency
Has America lost its humanity?
Kids kept in cages at the border
Shamefully, in the name of law and order

That's just one example of our divided state
Not enough love; far too much hate
An election year; a cause for hope
Sadly it looks like the answer's nope

G-d's given us each two big toes
Two eyes, two thumbs and two elbows
The grass is green; the sky is blue
Do they look the same to me and you?

I'm black; you're white
Will we ever stop our fight?
He's gay; she's straight
One day might they double date?

She's young; he's old
Deaf to the story his life told
She's born rich; he's born poor
Should he remain so evermore?

Liberals; conservatives
Seems an ever widening bridge
Increasingly the activists
Have no tolerance for different politics

If I win must you lose?
Must we always have to choose?
Global Warming, let me guess
Is it real? Is it too late to fix this mess?

This country has freedom of religion
So why no room for division?
Raised with a set of beliefs
Must we give all others grief?

Immigration has become a call to arms
But is it really a source of harm?
My neighbors all have guns
Should I feel safe or prepare to run?

Yes, the country seems in an ugly state
Where's the love? Why the hate?
Yes, two thumbs for everyone
Are they really better placed on some?

Now a pandemic has reached our shores
It should unite us but it has divided us even more
We have all witnessed the 2020 result
Sadly, a year that's proved most costly and difficult

To me Trump certainly bears the bulk of the blame
The issues that divide us he most surely inflamed
And he underestimated the scope of the virus's reach
And its seriousness he denied in his every speech

The works that follow focus on the virus for sure
And Trump's impact on it and on so much more
Black Lives Matter, schooling and voting too
So read on if interested or if you have nothing better to do!

The "Temporary" New Normal

Silence - not the sound of a single bouncing ball
Not off the floor, a racket, or a wall
The Corona virus is here in force
And no one seemed certain of its strength or course

The Feds send mixed messages and have been slow to act
Confusion, not solutions, seems the fact
The states, cities and towns on their own
Social distancing and social contact suggested only by phone

First, case tracking and containment was the goal
But all too quickly cases rose to an unmanageable toll
Widespread testing, self isolation the need
Time for every citizen to do their part and take heed

Sporting events were some of the first to self isolate
Soon after all forms of entertainment shut their gates
Colleges sent students home for Spring break
Or for the remainder of the Spring semester for safety sake

And it seems young children weren't really taking ill
But there were fears that they were carriers still
So slowly but surely schools at all levels were being closed
For how long and to what effect it's hard to know

Seniors and those with pre-existing conditions most at risk
Both to contract the virus and get very very sick
Respiratory illness is the main result of the disease
Symptoms - fever, shortness of breath, coughing and sneeze

The U.S. is certainly not alone in this plight
First China, then Europe, have been stricken with this blight
U.S. citizens working or vacationing in a foreign place
Are now scrambling to get back into the States

The economics of this pandemic are clearly staggering
The markets are experiencing wild daily swings
Commerce of all kinds is slowing to a crawl
A sharp recession coming soon is a most likely call

Food and household essentials have flown off store shelves
A clear early sign of panic folks can see for themselves
And still the President's false reassurances help us not a bit
Just more lies he spews for his own benefit

The confusion he recklessly caused at airport border controls
Thousands waited packed like sardines
for hours if the truth be told
And promise after promise for more testing to come
But waiting in line for miles surely didn't look much like fun

We're still just at the beginning of this horrible event
Cracks in our social fabric will become more and more evident
We're still just at the beginning; give that some thought
A few weeks; a few months; how long till we're all overwrought

I wish I had more faith in our country's leadership
To be able to steer us through this prolonged hardship
While I pray they step up to the challenges ahead
I fear I can only rely on my family, my friends and myself instead

No Twilight Zone Please

Well, I have on my mask and my gloves
To protect me and all those I love
I talk to my children and friends on the phone
Helps me from feeling so very very alone

Curl up with the TV and a good book
Hell, even help my wife clean and cook
Downloaded the movie Groundhog Day
Hey, that's our reality what can I say

Springtime and the weather's getting nice
On rainy days we really pay a price
Because on nice days we go out and walk
A nice pace, we hold hands and talk

Can't watch the news on TV at night
In the evening I really prefer something light
The news, rightfully so, is focused on one thing
The virus, and that news is all too frightening

My wife has found some salvation on the net
Several on-line games she's been able to get
Her friends are able to get on-line with her too
A way for them to connect; to have something to do

My children, grandchildren do their work from home
Probably a lot more productive than me writing poems
We each do what we need to do, whatever we can
And they read my stuff, you know, to quiet the "old man"

This quarantine is really only two plus weeks old
And it's just the beginning we're being told
I wonder how many husbands and wives
Are secreting away some sharp kitchen knives

Actually, that's not something to kid about
Guns and bullets have nearly been sold out
Sure, they were bought to defend and protect
But they easily could produce a very different effect

Science continues to research and learn all that it can
To come up with a good medical plan
And ramping up needed medical supplies
And placing more first responders on the front lines

Despite those efforts the numbers keep getting worse
Putting us all on a possible disastrous course
The day may be coming when doctors must pick
Who will get treatment if and when we get sick

Meanwhile we continue practicing social distancing
That's our part to help contain this thing
I'll do my best and I think my family and friends will too
Until we all see this deadly virus thing through

So for now we'll just go on day after day
But just how long can we all keep going this way
I hope there isn't a Twilight Zone plot just around the bend
And all the scary possible things one might portend

Health v. Wealth

In one corner we have our wealth
And in the other we have our health
It seems they may be destined for a fight
Really? And so really which one is right

Day after day the markets climbed high
Almost hit thirty K; just a drop shy
Then the virus shut commerce down
Empty stores, streets, cities and towns

Social distancing was mandated to flatten the curve
This mandate we were all required to observe
Business could operate with workers off site
But for many that solution wasn't at all right

Consumer spending makes our economy go
With folks staying home things just had to slow
The DOW dropped below nineteen K
My G-d take action; please save the day!

You see, at the very beginning of all this
The President they charged, the virus he dismissed
It's a hoax Democrats invented just to hurt him
Heed not those scientific predictions so grim

But soon the numbers belied those false facts
Rapidly spreading by people to people contact
Soon the sick would overwhelm health resources
Thus requiring mandating a rather drastic course

Keep people at a safe distance apart
Six feet of separation seemed a good start
Gatherings of no more than two fifty at first
Then fifty, then ten; the number of sick are getting worse

These measures deemed necessary to flatten the curve
But it seemed the President's agenda was not being served
A robust economy was his best argument
For his being re-elected as president

So without any facts or scientific evidence
He blatantly put forth this utter nonsense
By Easter, two short weeks hence,
Normal business and social operations will commence

Now understand that at the same time of his decree
Health care experts staunchly disagreed
New cases and deaths were still rapidly on the rise
Which is why his position was so soundly criticized

But to be fair Trump's voice is not the only voice
Many others would relax controls if given the choice
Fear of recession or worse on so many minds
A two plus trillion relief bill the President signed

So with new outbreaks in the Southern Hemisphere
As those countries approach the Fall time of year
And rising cases in Europe and here at home
And so little about this virus really known

With little chance for a vaccine within a year
And with little empirical data let's be clear
With testing far, far lagging case results
All these reasons makes decisions difficult

So what are our leaders to do
I just pray they thoughtfully think this through
And don't just open the gates on an arbitrary date
And yes, if warranted, take some time and wait

Corona Virus Hallelujah
(A Tribute to Leonard Cohen)

We're stuck in the house both night and day
No hope anytime to get away
Like me, is this pandemic getting to you
If the TV's broke, I'll have a stroke
I'm so depressed, a total mess
Perhaps I should pray saying Hallelujah

Hallelujah,Hallelujah, Hallelujah, Hallelujah

I wear a mask when I shop for food
People there seem in an awful mood
Like them, is this pandemic getting to you
The things we need; they're grabbed with greed
And being smart staying six feet apart
I'm sweating just relaying this ordeal to you

Hallelujah, Hallelujah, Hallelujah, Hallelujah

No concerts, sports or even Broadway
Movies only watched at home these days
Lonely, is this pandemic getting to you
We take long walks; good time to talk
Unless it rains; that's such a pain
Now the parks are all closed up to you

Hallelujah, Hallelujah, Hallelujah, Hallelujah

The President they say is spewing lies again
Can't the man see what's coming around the bend
Don't let the politics of this virus fool you
Science must win; test each citizen
Social distance, with persistence
That formula will best protect me and you

Hallelujah, Hallelujah, Hallelujah, Hallelujah

Right now I can't see this virus end
No rainbow waiting around the bend
I wish I had some better news to give you
But I have my health; can't worry about wealth
My family's fine; we talk all the time
For that blessing here's one last HALLELUJAH

When This Is Done

So, what must we do when this pandemic's done
For many it's to go out and just have some fun
Or like me, give my family members each a big hug
When we're finally or temporarily rid of this bug

I'd like to see life return to some form of normalcy
To see folks able to walk outside constraint free
To see businesses and their staffs back at work
And kids in classrooms doing their schoolwork

To ride a bus, train or plane without fear
Without shunning folks who come too near
To see a movie at a theater on a big screen
With popcorn from the theater's popcorn machine

To see sports leagues and events restart their games
And Broadway theaters do the same
To dine out with my wife and some good friends
And help neighborhood shops and restaurants start to mend

To just sit in a coffee shop and have a brew
And watch the customers as they pass through
To get our social groups and clubs back together
To play sports or games or just whatever

And let's not forget those healthcare professionals
Who throughout this fight saved so many with their skills
And give generously to charities like the Red Cross
Which were depleted helping stem our collective loss

To judge our many leaders both good and bad
Who raised us up or proved embarrassingly sad
To not forget the media and the scientists
Who told the truth though the truth some tried to resist

But mostly this is what we must do right away
And not put it off for some other day
Make note of what we did right and what we did wrong
And do now what should have been done all along

We need to learn from these costly mistakes
And plan and do whatever it takes
Because there is one thing of which I have no doubt
History will repeat if we haven't worked solutions out

Our Staycation

The Corona Virus is not going away any time soon
For months we've been confined to the house - to a few rooms
At first the restrictions were State imposed
It was what it was; everything was closed

But little by little restrictions loosened up
And along with that things started to open up
First parks, then beaches, then outdoor dining
But folks wanted more so there was considerable whining

Young folks particularly keep pushing for more
With few places to go they congregated at the shore
The Governor fearful our good numbers would start to slip
Once again took strong steps to right the ship

Indoor dining which in a few days was set to restart
Is just one victim of the Governor's change of heart
And he won't announce any future reopening dates
How long does he expect us to just sit home and wait?

The economy has tanked; small businesses have closed
Many have gone bankrupt and many others foreclosed
Unemployment has skyrocketed right through the roof
Personal wealth for many has simply gone poof

All this is simply background for my "Staycation" story
The star, of course, is my wife in all her glory
She refused to let this virus and its effects win
And for sure she refuses to let it keep us in

Of course, she doesn't propose anything risky
No plane trips or cruises or other things chancy
She's found plenty to do that gets us out of the house
Her only deterrent is when I sometimes grouse

We walked the parks when very few ventured out
Before beaches were open we went there and walked about
We played golf the very first week of its restart
And did outdoor dining staying six feet apart

At Avon we found a great place to sit on the boards
That is until the cops kicked us off - some reward
Undaunted she had us back there again and again
We successfully stayed maybe five times out of ten

When we got bounced we went to Bradley instead
A very nice pavilion provided shade for our heads
And we found a very nice place to sit by the River Delaware
And no matter how hot, there was always a cool breeze there

As I write this she's out at the driving range
Out of the house and active once again for a change
Practicing for our golf date this coming Thursday
If it's to hot or it rains we'll find some other getaway

She does play games on-line with her friends
That's three days a week I have a chance to mend
But even on days when those games are through
She walks with me for two miles for something else to do

In addition, she's hard at work on our annual family album
She tries to avoid TV as the news makes her feel glum
She reads and chats with our son and daughter
And every day practices bridge come hell or high water

Now I'm not suggesting every activity or outing is a ten
But that doesn't stop us from trying something new
or doing it again
Because what's important is to get up and do
That's what helps us to see this pandemic through

So, if you feel stuck in the house with nothing to do
I hope this poem will inspire you
to find things you can safely do too
This pandemic, our new normal is here to stay
Take it from us, you can staycation safely and brighten your day

What A Time To Be Seventy-Five

Well, yes, I suppose it's good news we're still alive
But really, what a shitty time to be celebrating being seventy-five
With the virus affecting our nation's health and economy
Like so many others, my best days may well be behind me

A few years ago on my wife's 70th birthday we hosted this
wonderful day
A nice lunch with family and friends at a place overlooking
the bay
Bright sunshine, warm weather, everything just right
We'll cherish those memories, a day of delight

Celebrations today, if at all, must take a different form
A practice of keep away, social distance, must be the norm
By August folks may feel more comfortable gathered together
And preferably outside but we can't count on the weather

No, I can't see another party for her this year hosted by me
But frankly, the alternatives are few I can see
Trips by a plane or a cruise seem too big a risk to take
And at our age who needs to make a big mistake

So we're resigned to try to celebrate in a more modest way
Maybe a nice dinner with just family at a shore outdoor cafe
Or if it's raining on her birthday requiring a plan restart
Then in-doors with just the kids at tables spaced six feet apart

Graduations and weddings and all other important days
All need to be celebrated this year, if at all, in very modest ways
And most sadly too many untimely funerals only held on zoom
The saddest consequence of this pandemic; it can't end too soon

However we mark the occasion, a birthday is still just a day
I'm sure our family will help make it special some way
All of us together and healthy would be a very good start
In fact, all of us together and healthy would be the very best part

Back To School, Really?

We find ourselves in the heat of Summer
With virus cases escalating in numbers
And each passing day brings us closer
To an August or September school opener

Is it really right for schools to re-start?
In classrooms where kids learn science and the arts
Kids starting school as young as three
To post graduates seeking advanced degrees

There are private and there are public schools
Surely, not equipped with the same tools
Kids from affluent suburban towns
And those from inner cities that we've let down

Parents tired of homeschooling their kids
Wondering if enough was enough of what they did
And wanting, yes needing, to get back to work
Just back to some "normal"; we're all going berserk

Republican governors turning their heads
"So far not that many of our people are dead"
Democratic governors fighting the backlash
Folks wanting things open to start making cash

But did I mention virus cases are on the rise
That should come to no one as a surprise
More than half the country convinced it's a joke
A sinister Democratic Party hoax

Maybe the answer - split each full class into two halves
A smaller group could social distance in class
The other half could learn via zoom
And parallel the learning of the half in the room

And every other week the kids could trade places
That way teachers could connect with all of their faces
On the surface this may seem like a doable scheme
But a closer look reveals holes in this or any back to school dream

Shouldn't teachers, other staff, have a say in whatever's proposed
And what if all or part of the plan they oppose
And what if parents want to opt their kids out
Claiming their kids health and safety is what their objection's about

Is it healthy for kids to wear a mask in class all day
And possible to keep them apart in lunch lines and at play
And what's the protocol when one or two get sick
Schools better be able to address that issue quick

Testing, constant testing, must be a key plan component
But that said, we can't allow testing to make us over confident
How frequent to test; and how quick the result
Contact tracing, so critical, may prove to be difficult

Home to school and from school back to home
The number of contacts makes for a complex honeycomb
And staying ahead of a possible virus outbreak
Requires all involved the necessary precautions to take

Put the kids on a school or public bus
What could go wrong? What's the fuss?
How hard could it be to trace the virus back
To the source of a public bus initiated virus attack

And how should schools address extra-curricular activities
The spectrum runs from normal activities to a total freeze
I suppose the answer lies somewhere in-between
But adds concern when groups are permitted to convene

College presents some unique complexity
Young adults on their own and set free
While many will stay home and zoom their classes
Others will choose on campus or off campus houses

So let's get those college kids on a plane
Flying them to school sounds perfectly sane
Mix them together in dorms and classrooms
And any risks to them the schools will make them assume

We've seen what young folks on their own can be like
News reports of their behavior gives us old folks a fright
College profs and admins must be dreading the day
When they're surrounded by folks who act this way

And let's remember that colleges are businesses too
So parents are smart to be cautious of what they say to do
For good or bad they rely on sports revenues
And football, a Fall sport, may further cloud their view

If all this is not complicated enough
The President is making things doubly tough
Trump, they say, denies the virus is in any way a threat
This is a key component of his re-election bet

So he's a leader in the pressure to open things up
With any false science his team can dream up
"Ninety-nine percent of all cases are mild"
"And stop the testing; you're driving us wild"

And here's a last but important fact
A number of states have had to pull back
Just opening things up a little bit
Has spiked their cases they had to admit

And sports teams trying to restart their seasons
Have provided us the many reasons
Why starting at a time the virus is on the rise
Is anything but something wise

So what's the likely result if states open schools
That's a huge leap do not be fooled
Maybe we should wait a while
Until a vaccine or at least a vaccine trial

Or at least till folks take seriously minding
Wearing masks and social distancing
And follow science and not political spin
Maybe then schools can safely again begin

The Science

The Corona virus pandemic has brought science to the fore
And with it public scientific debate like never before
On the one hand are the science deniers
On the other, the believers who call the others liars

The recognized experts like Dr. Fauci and Dr. Birx
Apparently have been caught up in virus politics
Fauci was the first to be bounced from the task force
And most of America considered that a great loss

Dr. Birx hung in with the president's task force longer
Until Trump mentioned ingesting bleach or something stronger
On TV Dr. Gupta and others provided reason and facts
While Trump recruited doctors who some labeled quacks

The president's task force was led by none other than Mike Pence
And that choice alone should have told us
the effort made no sense
The briefings got briefer and finally totally disappeared
Trump's personal performance faltered
resulting in questions not cheers

Among the "remedies" Trump was quick to tout
Hydroxychloroquine was one he was most raving about
No scientific evidence could be found to support this "cure"
Nonetheless, millions of Trumpsters bought it out of the stores

In Trump's zeal to support the economy and his re-election
He promised a vaccine by September to hold Wall Street's attention
But as time continued to pass by from May to the Fall
It became clear it would be the end of the year if this year at all

Some six companies or more raced to create a vaccine
Their efforts for the most part to the public were unseen
And as one trial after another fell by the way
The public came to realize to expect a long delay

As time went by and the virus state by state grew
The more his detractors pointed out he had not a clue what to do
And the closer time crept to Election Day
The more they said he lied and denied science
to try to wish it away

Finally, his behavior led to him and his family catching the virus
He had the luxury of a team of doctors making a fuss
And experimental treatments not available to us all
Were part of the many medical advantages at his beck and call

And when he recovered he reverted to the old
Claiming this virus is no worse than a common cold
And really that not many people actually die
What about the two hundred thousand who in cemeteries lie

And all the while the pandemic was of the greatest concern
He was in court trying to get Obamacare overturned
A cornerstone of that law is protecting pre-existing conditions
Outrageous at this time to try to impose health care restrictions

Even if you're not a doctor or a science buff
A simple truth that's completely free of all that brainy stuff
Is wear a mask, wash your hands, and keep six feet apart
Do that and you'll be doing more than your part

Who Do You Call When Police MURDER?

Who do you call when police murder
Not Trump and probably not your governor
Who hears the voices, the pleas
Does anyone see us when we take a knee

Does anyone hear us when we chant
"Black Lives Matter" or is that an idle rant
How many George Floyds must die
Before we give love, not hate a try

How many marches, rallies and protests
Will it take to succeed in this quest
How many Ahmad Arberys must die
Till we broom sweep hate good-bye

In how many cities and states must we protest
Before we put discrimination to its final rest
How many Breonna Taylors must die
Before institutionalized oppression is vilified

How many slogans must we create
Four hundred years is too long a wait
"Standing in Solidarity"; "Black Lives Matter"
They have meaning, they're not idle chatter

For the very few Derek Chauvins caught and charged
Too many others are excused and their crimes discharged
The cops are not the only ones to blame
Too many of our leaders play the "fear the Black race" game

The Obama Presidency fermented the hate
The current administration fuels the hate mandate
"There were many good people on both sides."
One of the worst of the times Trump is said to have lied

I hope that as the demonstrations continue
That they're not giving the haters a new venue
The majority of white America supports the protests
But the violence scares them; it must be put to rest

Peaceful protests, sadly, have had only marginal effect
Rioting and looting, shameful, only lead to urban neglect
The VOTE is the best hope for lasting positive change
And the process fosters a civil, thoughtful exchange

Take this opportunity while you have the world's attention
Make signs, give speeches to this intention
To encourage every young person to register to vote
And those votes will be the reason
America sits up and takes note

The House of the Blacked Out Sun
(To the Tune of The House of the Rising Sun)

I named these verses done to a melody
The House of the Blacked Out Sun
My goal as you listen will be plain to see
It's to see that this administration is finally undone

In the White House in Washington town
A group of very bad people stay
Their goal is to bring the country down
And they will if we let them have their way

Mothers warn your children
Don't believe anything they say
They try to pit one group against another
That's how they work to have things their way

Trump is the leader of this divisive group
Pence, Barr, McConnell and others follow suit
And although it may be a dwindling group
Don't be fooled, their words and deeds pollute

So mothers hold tight to your children's hands
Make your voices heard and your votes be cast
Do your best, do it now, do all you can
To help ensure we've voted them out at last

My Country T'is Of Thee

My country t'is of thee
Should I stay or should I flee
The news gets worse every day
Can't trust anything Republicans say

The Donald sits on his throne
Texting insults on his phone
Nero simply turned his head
Trump encourages division to be spread

McConnell, Barr and others share the blame
Their conduct no less a shame
Where is a Morrow to call them out
Or even any Republican to raise some doubt

It's getting so close to the end of the year
And the worst may be before us I fear
Could Trump's re-election be a real thing
Imagine four more years of him in the West Wing

The Democrats wail and whine
But their sting so far has proved benign
The press continually reports breaking news
A phrase they very much abuse

So on and on it goes
Sin after sin gets exposed
To deflect, more and more outrageous lies
The media says he tells and then swears by

My country t'is of thee
This is sadly what I see
The Alt Right on the rise
Immigration criticized

The Corona virus out of control
All out efforts to cull the voter rolls
Voter suppression state by state
Gun deaths at an alarming rate

The social safely net under attack
Efforts to trim health care benefits back
BLM efforts to effect police reform
Turned into a law and order fear platform

The Republicans have now packed the Supreme Court
Assuring election issues would gain their support
If the Presidency, the Senate and the Court all go red
I fear our democracy may very well be dead

If this election doesn't turn the tide
There might not be anywhere to hide
And I may no longer be free to say
Out loud - there is a different way

When Did Voting Become So Difficult?

Well, it's just ten days until the election
My wife and I already have made our selections
We drove them directly to the official voting site
Checked and double checked to do everything right

In years past voting on Election Day
At your local school in person, people voted that way
The process was easy; a machine recorded your vote
And kept a tally; a permanent vote note

But this year almost all voting will be done by mail
The jury is out; will the process get a pass or a fail
There are several efforts underway to thwart its success
All intended to discredit the vote by mail process

In New Jersey all voters received a ballot by mail
Republicans sought any means those votes to curtail
They went to court to try to stop the mail-in vote process
Arguing mail in ballots would result in a fraudulent mess

They argued that voters should vote in person if possible
Where their eligibility to vote can be certified to be credible
But Covid has forced the State to limit public gatherings
And the courts agreed with the way the State sees things

Now Trump realized that a large voter turnout would be his demise
So his followers have sought any means possible to limit voter size
One such effort was to reduce the availability of US mail
Sorting machines, drop boxes and more were curtailed

In other states where Republicans were more in control
Several means were employed to reduce the voter roles
Early voting was reduced or not at all allowed
And voting sites were limited resulting in long lines, crowds

On TV there were reports of extremely long voter lines
Twelve hours or more standing in the hot sunshine
But Americans seem determined to vote and be heard
Republican efforts to thwart taken as challenging words

The heavier the turnout the worst the news for Trump
Now six days in a row he's out on the stump
Calling the election a hoax and a Democratic sham
All seemingly part of a continuing relentless flimflam

Trump they say may not accept the election results
If he loses it's just Democrats trying to insult
His latest effort is to "pack" the US Supreme Court
And hope they'll deliver a win with a packed court's support

A liberal voice and a lifelong women's rights advocate
That was Justice Ruth Bader Ginsburg's lifelong mandate
Her untimely death has allowed Republicans to pounce
And an ultra-conservative woman in her place to announce

They're rushing her through a high court confirmation
Much to Democrats' extreme consternation
Intent on getting her placed on the Court
So she's in place for any Biden win to abort

So, with all that going on I have serious doubts
That a fair election result can be brought about
No matter how many Democratic votes come in
The Republicans will find a way to rig a Trump win

And if by some chance the Democrats do win
It's likely Trump will still fight to stay in
His words may incite his base to riot and cause ruin
He may prolong and relish the chaos by not giving in

My wife and I have made a just in case plan
To go someplace far away like to the Isle of Man
Not forever mind you; that wouldn't work for us
No, just until President Harris can put an end to this muss

It's An Election Year and Things Are Heating Up!

Seventeen Republicans were once in the 2016 race
Each one seeking support of the base
We all bear witness to how badly that turned out
And sadly no hope for a 2020 turnabout

Trump is the Republican 2020 candidate
And Pence once again is his running mate
The Dems actually started with a larger field
And for a long time few of them were willing to yield

CNN and MSNBC constantly had them on
While on FOX they were relentlessly set upon
Slowly, the field was dwindled down
Until finally Joe Biden won the primary crown

All the while the Republican's new attack theme -
"Socialism" is the Democrat's dream
Cortez became the Republican's poster Dem
For everything that was wrong with them

Then after a long, some would say too long, wait
Biden announced his VP running mate
A gifted Kamala Harris, the California Senator
A woman, a minority, and a former prosecutor

So, now the 2020 presidential field was set
And right up to the election the winner was anyone's guess
The race was complicated by these major controversies
The virus, Black Lives Matter, and the economy

The Dems hammered and hammered on everything Trump said
And on his failure to contain the virus and all the resulting dead
And that he denied and flaunted the science
Further they suggested he acted without any conscience

The virus brought the economy front and center into play
Republicans and Democrats responding in starkly different ways
The Dems consistently putting public health and safety first
The Republicans claiming a stunted economy was worse

On so many related issues the sides were drawn
Republicans argued in school was where kids belonged
So the debate raged between in person learning and zoom
In the end kids were mostly "opted out' of the classroom

Science taught us wearing a mask was the best defense
And not wearing one made absolutely no sense
But Republicans led by Trump refused to wear a mask
Claiming giving up their rights was just too much to ask

And Black Lives Matter gave Republicans a new theme
Riots, looting, the death of the white suburbia dream
Biden, Harris, they'll unleash the urban hordes
Vote law and order Republicans across the board

So as November neared the race stayed hot
Voting took the center stage spot
Democrats pushed to get the vote out
Republicans used every means to turn off the spout

Key states like Florida, PA and Michigan remained in play
Wisconsin, too, right up to Election Day
And "toss up" Senate races that could shift the tide
From the Republican to the Democrat's side

It's still October and I have my fingers crossed
For America's sake this election won't be lost
The Dems will win the White House and more
And my family and I won't have to relocate off-shore

The Election, Finally?

Well, it's finally Election Day
And the voters have certainly had their say
Early and mail in voting set an all time high
And Election Day voters gave it a most serious try

And let's give credit to both Biden and Trump
Till the very end they worked hard on the stump
Battleground states saw both candidates a lot
As they both worked those "up for grabs" spots

Yes, it's certainly Election Day
But any results may be days or even weeks away
It may take awhile to call the race
And like everyone else I wish they'd pick up the pace

A quick and decisive end is Wall Street's bet
And gambling houses' bets too are all set
Their odds and their hopes favor Biden to win
I hope their predictions aren't wrong once again

This time around the news media is playing it safe
Even if it means not being first out of the gate
They've resisted making any pre-election predictions
And seem to be avoiding past election night traditions

Cities bracing for marches and riots
Extra cops to help assure things stay quiet
Store windows boarded up preparing for the worst
Doorways and stairways securely reinforced

And for weeks leading up to Election Day
Folks have been stocking up for come what may
Groceries and necessities flying off the shelves
Taking precautions to help safeguard themselves

Can you just picture the worldwide news
Shootings and riots if Trump should loose
And if by chance Trump should win
Protests and marches in the streets once again

I fear no matter when or what the result
The weeks following the decision will prove most difficult
Harsh words and incidents might fan the flames
With each side looking at the other to blame

And should the Supreme Court be brought into the mix
I hardly think that would be accepted as an appropriate fix
They might put a legal end to Biden's fate
But that would clearly not be the end of the debate

So as of this writing the results are not known
And maybe any further comments I should simply postpone
My family is prepared for the worst and hoping for the best
And until there's a result we'll stick very close to our nest

Looking Ahead

Well, on Saturday, Joe Biden was finally declared the winner
But truly the margin of victory couldn't have been thinner
And although Trump will employ every trick at his command
In the end it appears that none of his challenges will stand

Trump has claimed fraud in the counting everywhere
But despite their efforts all results have been found to be fair
True, some states like Georgia have ordered a recount
But it's highly unlikely those efforts will turn the election about

The election map of the US is starkly telling
Mostly Red from coast to coast so compelling
Dots of Blue representing the dense urban sites
Contrasting voter preference like day and night

Geography also contrasts voter choice
The Coasts, East and West, give Dems their voice
The South strongly prefers Republicans
The remaining states determine which party wins

This time Joe Biden squeezed out the win
Thanks to Rust Belt states like Michigan
The Southwest also helped get him over the top
The eleventh hour saw a number of states flip-flop

Here is a most important fact
Of which Joe Biden must never loose track
Comparing the votes in 2016 to today
Seven million more votes went Trump's way

In spite of misdeeds and lies they claim he has told
His base remains solidly in his fold
Biden begins his presidential term
With a nation's polarization so totally firm

So, based on the map and the voting too
Biden will have a lot of work ahead of him to do
To fulfill one of his key presidential goals
To be the president of the country as a whole

There are other results that have me scratching my head
The experts predicted Susan Collins' chances were dead
Nonetheless she won going away
Six more years in the Senate she'll stay

In South Carolina and Kentucky the Dems spent a ton
In a losing effort to see McConnell and Graham undone
McConnell won re-election in a huge way
He'll feel empowered to obstruct Biden each and every day

As of this writing the Senate has not been settled
Runoff elections in Georgia still to be vetted
Should those elections not happen to go the Dems way
Obstruction and gridlock may be the order of the day

So, in a lot of ways the Obama years may likely be repeated
Having both Dems and Republicans in the halls of power seated
The challenge for Biden and the House will be
To find some compromises with the Senate, hopefully

Meanwhile disruptions continue on our streets
Quieting them will be a challenge Biden needs to meet
Peaceful assembly and protest is an American right
But not rioting, looting and more all through the night

Dealing with the virus was a campaign promise
To not tackle it right away would be quite remiss
A promised national mask mandate may very well be tried
But state by state its acceptance might well be denied

The departments of government need to be redone
Starting with Cabinet appointments since Biden has won
And where compromise with the Senate fails
Executive orders to undo all of Trump's many ails

Populate his staff and administration
With diversity representative of the people of this nation
Give Dreamers a path to become citizens
And an immigration policy with fairness built in

Let the Russians know quite clearly where he stands
And re-establish America's fine international brand
Let both Canada and Mexico know
Among us free trade and commerce should flow

Oh, there is so much Biden will need to get done
Things to be fixed, undone, and new things begun
Like restoring credibility to the justice system
Such a disgrace under Trump and Barr what it has become

Looking ahead I could go on surmising so much more
And predicting all the things that might be in store
But I'd be overlooking the most important thing
The sheer optimism a Biden presidency should bring

So I'll just end this work at this spot
Well, with this one little caveat
I'm sure next year there promises to be
An avalanche of happenings to follow for you and me

About The Author

Steve Rosen is a retired attorney who lives with his wife Marilyn of fifty plus years in their long time residence in New Jersey.

Steve has two children and four grandchildren. Most of his poetry centers on his family and thoughts about the world around him.

All of his works rhyme.

About The Book

Steve Rosen did not set out to write *2020: A Perspective in Rhyme*, but as the events of the now-infamous year grew, the work developed into a collection of rhymes and verses chronicling the strangeness, absurdity, growth, and tragedy that was the year 2020. Central to the work is the COVID-19 pandemic, with Rosen illustrating the controversy surrounding science, the restrictions placed for its containment, the health versus wealth debate, and whether schools should remain open, online, or both. His poetry focuses on people, politics—one important component being the 2020 election—and the rise of the Black Lives Matter movement.

Rosen's collection of rhymes regarding 2020 is powerful, emotional, and important for generations to come to understand the chaotic year that was 2020.